Rooney

by Iain Gray

Lang**Syne**

PUBLISHING

WRITING *to* REMEMBER

Lang**Syne**

PUBLISHING

WRITING *to* REMEMBER

Vineyard Business Centre,
Pathhead, Midlothian EH37 5XP
Tel: 01875 321 203 Fax: 01875 321 233
E-mail: info@lang-syne.co.uk
www.langsyneshop.co.uk

Design by Dorothy Meikle
Printed by Ricoh Print Scotland
© Lang Syne Publishers Ltd 2011

ISBN 978-1-85217-337-1

Rooney

MOTTO:
Always faithful to friends.

CREST:
A naked arm, the hand grasping a sword.

NAME variations include:
Ó Ruanaidh (*Gaelic*)
O'Roney
O'Rooney
Roonay
Roney
Roony

Chapter one:

Origins of Irish surnames

According to an old saying, there are two types of Irish – those who actually are Irish and those who wish they were.

This sentiment is only one example of the allure that the high romance and drama of the proud nation's history holds for thousands of people scattered across the world today.

It's a sad fact, however, that the vast majority of Irish surnames are found far beyond Irish shores, rather than on the Emerald Isle itself.

The population stood at around eight million souls in 1841, but today it stands at fewer than six million.

This is mainly a tragic consequence of the potato famine, also known as the Great Hunger, which devastated Ireland between 1845 and 1849.

The Irish peasantry had become almost wholly reliant for basic sustenance on the potato, first introduced from the Americas in the seventeenth century.

When the crop was hit by a blight, at least 800,000 people starved to death while an estimated two million others were forced to seek a new life far from their native shores – particularly in America, Canada, and Australia.

The effects of the potato blight continued until about 1851, by which time a firm pattern of emigration had become established.

Ireland's loss, however, was to the gain of the countries in which the immigrants settled, contributing enormously, as their descendants do today, to the well being of the nations in which their forefathers settled.

But those who were forced through dire circumstance to establish a new life in foreign parts never forgot their roots, or the proud heritage and traditions of the land that gave them birth.

Nor do their descendants.

It is a heritage that is inextricably bound up in the colourful variety of Irish names themselves – and the origin and history of these names forms an integral part of the vibrant drama that is the nation's history, one of both glorious fortune and tragic misfortune.

This history is well documented, and one of the most important and fascinating of the earliest sources are *The Annals of the Four Masters*, compiled between 1632 and 1636 by four friars at the Franciscan Monastery in County Donegal.

Compiled from earlier sources, and purporting to go back to the Biblical Deluge, much of the material takes in the mythological origins and history of Ireland and the Irish.

This includes tales of successive waves of invaders and settlers such as the Fomorians, the Partholonians, the Nemedians, the Fir Bolgs, the Tuatha De Danann, and the Laigain.

Of particular interest are the *Milesian Genealogies*,

because the majority of Irish clans today claim a descent from either Heremon, Ir, or Heber – three of the sons of Milesius, a king of what is now modern day Spain.

These sons invaded Ireland in the second millennium B.C, apparently in fulfilment of a mysterious prophecy received by their father.

This Milesian lineage is said to have ruled Ireland for nearly 3,000 years, until the island came under the sway of England's King Henry II in 1171 following what is known as the Cambro-Norman invasion.

This is an important date not only in Irish history in general, but for the effect the invasion subsequently had for Irish surnames.

'Cambro' comes from the Welsh, and 'Cambro-Norman' describes those Welsh knights of Norman origin who invaded Ireland.

But they were invaders who stayed, inter-marrying with the native Irish population and founding their own proud dynasties that bore Cambro-Norman names such as Archer, Barbour, Brannagh, Fitzgerald, Fitzgibbon, Fleming, Joyce, Plunkett, and Walsh – to name only a few.

These 'Cambro-Norman' surnames that still flourish throughout the world today form one of the three main categories in which Irish names can be placed – those of Gaelic-Irish, Cambro-Norman, and Anglo-Irish.

Previous to the Cambro-Norman invasion of the twelfth century, and throughout the earlier invasions and settlement of those wild bands of sea rovers known as the Vikings in the eighth and ninth centuries, the population of the island was relatively small, and it was normal for a person to be identified through the use of only a forename.

But as population gradually increased and there were many more people with the same forename, surnames were adopted to distinguish one person, or one community, from another.

Individuals identified themselves with their own particular tribe, or 'tuath', and this tribe – that also became known as a clann, or clan – took its name from some distinguished ancestor who had founded the clan.

The Gaelic-Irish form of the name Kelly, for example, is Ó Ceallaigh, or O'Kelly, indicating descent from an original 'Ceallaigh', with the 'O' denoting 'grandson of.' The name was later anglicised to Kelly.

The prefix 'Mac' or 'Mc', meanwhile, as with the clans of the Scottish Highlands, denotes 'son of.'

Although the Irish clans had much in common with their Scottish counterparts, one important difference lies in what are known as 'septs', or branches, of the clan.

Septs of Scottish clans were groups who often bore an entirely different name from the clan name but were under the clan's protection.

In Ireland, septs were groups that shared the same name and who could be found scattered throughout the four provinces of Ulster, Leinster, Munster, and Connacht.

The 'golden age' of the Gaelic-Irish clans, infused as their veins were with the blood of Celts, pre-dates the Viking invasions of the eighth and ninth centuries and the Norman invasion of the twelfth century, and the sacred heart of the country was the Hill of Tara, near the River Boyne, in County Meath.

Known in Gaelic as 'Teamhar na Rí', or Hill of Kings, it was the royal seat of the 'Ard Rí Éireann', or High King of Ireland, to whom the petty kings, or chieftains, from the island's provinces were ultimately subordinate.

It was on the Hill of Tara, beside a stone pillar known as the Irish 'Lia Fáil', or Stone of Destiny, that the High Kings were inaugurated and, according to legend, this stone would emit a piercing screech that could be heard all over Ireland when touched by the hand of the rightful king.

The Hill of Tara is today one of the island's main tourist attractions.

Opposition to English rule over Ireland, established in the wake of the Cambro-Norman invasion, broke out frequently and the harsh solution adopted by the powerful forces of the Crown was to forcibly evict the native Irish from their lands.

These lands were then granted to Protestant colonists, or 'planters', from Britain.

Many of these colonists, ironically, came from Scotland and were the descendants of the original 'Scotti', or 'Scots', who gave their name to Scotland after migrating there in the fifth century A.D., from the north of Ireland.

Colonisation entailed harsh penal laws being imposed on the majority of the native Irish population, stripping them practically of all of their rights.

The Crown's main bastion in Ireland was Dublin and its environs, known as the Pale, and it was the dispossessed peasantry who lived outside this Pale, desperately striving to eke out a meagre living.

It was this that gave rise to the modern-day expression of someone or something being 'beyond the pale'.

Attempts were made to stamp out all aspects of the ancient Gaelic-Irish culture, to the extent that even to bear a Gaelic-Irish name was to invite discrimination.

This is why many Gaelic-Irish names were anglicised with, for example, and noted above, Ó Ceallaigh, or O'Kelly, being anglicised to Kelly.

Succeeding centuries have seen strong revivals of Gaelic-Irish consciousness, however, and this has led to many families reverting back to the original form of their name, while the language itself is frequently found on the fluent tongues of an estimated 90,000 to 145,000 of the island's population.

Ireland's turbulent history of religious and political strife is one that lasted well into the twentieth century, a landmark century that saw the partition of the island into the twenty-six counties of the independent Republic of

Ireland, or Eire, and the six counties of Northern Ireland, or Ulster.

Dublin, originally founded by Vikings, is now a vibrant and truly cosmopolitan city while the proud city of Belfast is one of the jewels in the crown of Ulster.

It was Saint Patrick who first brought the light of Christianity to Ireland in the fifth century A.D.

Interpretations of this Christian message have varied over the centuries, often leading to bitter sectarian conflict – but the many intricately sculpted Celtic Crosses found all over the island are symbolic of a unity that crosses the sectarian divide.

It is an image that fuses the 'old gods' of the Celts with Christianity.

All the signs from the early years of this new millennium indicate that sectarian strife may soon become a thing of the past – with the Irish and their many kinsfolk across the world, be they Protestant or Catholic, finding common purpose in the rich tapestry of their shared heritage.

Chapter two:

Ancient roots

**Present day County Down in Ulster, which along with
Munster, Leinster and Connacht is one of the four
ancient provinces of the Emerald Isle, is the original
territory of the proud clan of Rooney – known in Gaelic-
Irish as Ó Ruanaidh.**

The name means 'descendant of the champion' and, in
common with many other native Irish clans, the ancestry of
the Rooneys is truly illustrious, descended as they are from
one of Ireland's earliest royal dynasties.

The origins and lives of times of the island's first
inhabitants are steeped in myth and legend, and it is
according to legend that the first tribe to inhabit the land was
the Fomorians although, rather improbably, they are said to
have dwelled mainly in the sea.

Invasion then came in the form of the Partholonians
who, after a bitter and bloody struggle for supremacy over
the Fomorians that lasted close on 300 years, were wiped
out in an epidemic.

Then came the tribe of the Nemed, followed by the Fir
Bolgs who, after inter-marrying with the Fomorians, held
sway over the island until the arrival at an undetermined
date of the Tuatha De Danann.

There then followed the era of the Milesian invaders,

and the ancestry of the Rooneys can be tracked back through the dim mists of time to Ireland's Milesian monarchs.

It was Heremon, Heber, Ir and Amergin – sons of Milesius, a king of what is now modern day Spain, who had planned to invade the Emerald Isle in fulfilment of a mysterious Druidic prophecy.

Milesius died before he could embark on the invasion but his sons successfully undertook the daunting task in his stead in about 1699 B.C.

Legend holds that their invasion fleet was scattered in a storm and Ir killed when his ship was driven onto the island of Scellig-Mhicheal, off the coast of modern day Co. Kerry.

Only Heremon, Heber and Amergin survived, although Ir left issue.

Heremon and Heber became the first of the Milesian monarchs of Ireland, but Heremon later killed Heber in a quarrel said to have been caused by their wives, while Amergin was slain by Heremon in an argument over territory.

The Co. Down barony of Iveagh became the main territory of the Rooney descendants of the Milesian monarchs, and it was here that they were proudly styled 'Lords of Iveagh' – with the modern day parish of Ballroney, in the Iveagh barony recalling the early presence there of the clan.

Maintaining their hold on this territory involved frequent recourse to arms, but the Rooneys also distinguished themselves as accomplished bards, or poets.

The bardic institution was rooted in Celtic custom, with the bards performing the important role of custodians of a clan's heritage and traditions.

On many a cold winter night, gathered around a blazing fire, the clan would be treated by the bard to stirring tales of the daring deeds of their ancestors.

In the late seventeenth century, in a bid to stamp out all vestiges of Gaelic-Irish culture, the forces of the Crown outlawed the bardic institution – but the tradition was so deeply rooted in the Gaelic-Irish psyche that it has continued to thrive and survive to this day.

One celebrated Rooney bard – so renowned that he was known as the Chief Poet of Ireland – was the late eleventh century Ceallach O'Rooney.

But the Rooney bards did not solely serve their own clan. In common with other bards they also fulfilled the important and honoured role as hereditary bards of other clans – one example being Eoin O'Rooney, the late fourteenth century hereditary bard of the McGuinnesses.

In a much later century, and continuing the literary tradition of the Rooneys, William Rooney, born in Dublin in 1873 and who died in 1901, was the journalist and poet who served as the first chairman of the prestigious Celtic Literary Society.

The fact that the Rooneys served as bards to other clans explains the presence of some of their descendants far beyond the original territory of Co. Down.

But at least one family of the Rooney name appears to have been quite separate from the Rooneys of Co. Down.

These were Rooneys who took their name from Maolruandha Mór, a brother of Conchobhar, a late tenth century king of Connacht.

It is from this sept that the names of O'Mulrooney and Mulroony derive.

The Rooneys also distinguished themselves in the ecclesiastical sphere, with Felix O'Rooney serving as an early thirteenth century Archbishop of Tuam, in Co. Galway.

The Annals of the Four Masters state of him: 'Felix O'Rooney, Archbishop of Tuam, after having some time before resigned his bishopric for the sake of God, and after having assumed the monastic habit in Kilmurry Mary's Abbey, in Dublin, died.'

He died in 1238, and had apparently been imprisoned for a time by the O'Connors after incurring the wrath of the powerful clan for reasons that remain unclear.

It was an O'Connor, meanwhile, who became embroiled in a bloody power struggle that was to lead to arguably the most momentous event in Ireland's long and turbulent history.

This was an event that had truly dire consequences not

only for the O'Connors but also for all other native Irish clans – not least the Rooneys.

Twelfth century Ireland was far from being a unified nation, split up as it was into territories ruled over by squabbling chieftains who ruled as kings in their own right – and this inter-clan rivalry worked to the advantage of the invaders. In a series of bloody conflicts, one chieftain, or king, would occasionally gain the upper hand over his rivals, and by 1156 the most powerful was Muirchertach MacLochlainn, King of the O'Neills.

The equally powerful Rory O'Connor, King of the O'Connors of Connacht, opposed him but he increased his power and influence by allying himself with Dermot MacMurrough, King of Leinster.

MacLochlainn and MacMurrough were aware that the main key to the kingdom of Ireland was the thriving trading port of Dublin that had been established by invading Vikings, or Ostmen, in 852 A.D.

Their combined forces took Dublin, but when MacLochlainn died the Dubliners rose up in revolt and overthrew the unpopular MacMurrough.

A triumphant Rory O'Connor now entered Dublin and was later inaugurated as Ard Rí, but MacMurrough was not one to humbly accept defeat.

He appealed for help from England's Henry II in unseating O'Connor, an act that was to radically affect the future course of Ireland's fortunes.

Chapter three:

Rebel cause

The English monarch agreed to help MacMurrough, but distanced himself from direct action by delegating his Norman subjects in Wales with the task.

These ambitious and battle-hardened barons and knights had first settled in Wales following the Norman Conquest of England in 1066 and, with an eye on rich booty, plunder and lands, were only too eager to obey their sovereign's wishes and furnish MacMurrough with aid.

MacMurrough crossed the Irish Sea to Bristol, where he rallied powerful barons such as Robert Fitzstephen and Maurice Fitzgerald to his cause, along with Gilbert de Clare, Earl of Pembroke.

As an inducement to de Clare, MacMurrough offered him the hand of his beautiful young daughter, Aife, in marriage, with the further sweetener to the deal that he would take over the province of Leinster on MacMurrough's death.

The mighty Norman war machine soon moved into action, and so fierce and disciplined was their onslaught on the forces of O'Connor and his allies that by 1171 they had re-captured Dublin, in the name of MacMurrough, and other strategically important territories.

Henry II now began to take cold feet over the venture,

realising that he may have created a rival in the form of a separate Norman kingdom in Ireland.

Accordingly, he landed on the island, near Waterford, at the head of a large army with the aim of curbing the power of his barons.

But protracted war between the King and his barons was averted when they submitted to the royal will, promising homage and allegiance in return for holding the territories they had conquered in the King's name.

Henry also received the submission and homage of many of the Irish chieftains, tired as they were with internecine warfare and also perhaps realising that as long as they were rivals and not united they were no match for the powerful forces the English Crown could muster.

English dominion over Ireland was ratified through the Treaty of Windsor of 1175, under the terms of which Rory O'Connor, for example, was only allowed to rule territory unoccupied by the Normans in the role of a vassal of the king.

This humiliation appears to have been too much for the proud O'Connor to bear, for he abdicated his kingship and took himself off to monastic seclusion.

He died in 1198, the last in a line of no less than eleven O'Connor High Kings of Ireland.

Further waves of ambitious Anglo-Norman adventurers descended on the island, leading to the creation of three 'separate' Irelands.

There were the territories of the privileged and powerful

barons and their retainers, the Ireland of the disaffected Gaelic-Irish who held lands unoccupied by the Normans, and the Pale – comprised of Dublin itself and a substantial area of its environs ruled over by an English elite.

It was a recipe for rebellion, with the island frequently torn apart in succeeding centuries as native Irish such as the Rooneys fought with bloody determination in defence of their ancient rights and freedom.

Exacerbating the rapid decline in fortunes of the Irish clans was the policy of settling, or 'planting' loyal Protestants on their land – a policy that started during the reign from 1491 to 1547 of Henry VIII, whose Reformation effectively outlawed the established Roman Catholic faith throughout his dominions.

This settlement of loyal Protestants continued through-out the subsequent reigns of Elizabeth I, James I (James VI of Scotland), and Charles I.

The Rooney province of Ulster became the launch pad in 1595 for what is known to Irish history as *Cogadh na Naoi mBliama*, or the Nine Years War – a war in which the Rooneys found themselves, along with other Ulster clans, in rebellious alliance with the more powerful O'Neills and O'Donnells.

Following a number of spectacular victories over the forces of the Crown, the rebels were decisively beaten at the battle of Kinsale in 1601 and the rebellion finally suppressed three years later.

In September of 1607, in what is known as The Flight of the Earls, Hugh O'Neill, 2nd Earl of Tyrone and Rory O'Donnell, 1st Earl of Tyrconnel, sailed into foreign exile from the village of Rathmullan, on the shore of Lough Swilly, in Co. Donegal, accompanied by ninety loyal followers.

For many historians this event marked the final collapse of the ancient Gaelic order.

The suppression of the rebellion and the flight of its leaders paved the way for the Plantation of Ulster, with the Rooneys and other native Irish clans being dispossessed of their lands.

The province had proven stubbornly resistant to English invasion, and it was in a bid to stamp out rebellion once and for all that English and Scottish Protestants were 'planted' on land confiscated from Irish Catholic landowners.

The main landowners in Ulster became known as Undertakers, because they had to undertake to import tenants from their own estates in Scotland and England.

Another group known as Servitors, because they had served the cause of the Crown in suppressing the rebellion, were also granted land.

These Planters were forbidden to take on Irish tenants or sell their land to any Irishman – with the native Irish such as the Rooneys forced to settle near military garrisons and Protestant churches, with attempts made to convert Irish Catholics to the Protestant faith.

But these policies only served to fuel the flames of further rebellion, particularly in 1641, when Protestant settlers were driven from their lands.

Revenge came in 1649 in the form of England's 'Lord Protector', Oliver Cromwell, who brutally suppressed the rebellion.

The northeastern town of Drogheda, for example, was stormed and taken in September of 1649 and between 2,000 and 4,000 of its inhabitants killed, including priests who were summarily put to the sword.

The defenders of the town's St. Peter's Church, who had refused to surrender, were burned to death as they huddled for refuge in the steeple and the church was deliberately torched.

A similar fate awaited Wexford, in the southeast, where at least 1,500 of its inhabitants were slaughtered, including 200 defenceless women, despite their pathetic pleas for mercy.

Catholic landowners in Ulster, Leinster and Munster had their lands confiscated and grudgingly given pathetically small estates west of the river Shannon – where they were hemmed in by colonies of Cromwellian soldiers and other settlers.

An edict was issued that any native Irish found east of the River Shannon after May 1, 1654, faced either summary execution or transportation to the West Indies.

The final nail in the coffin of the Gaelic-Irish came

through what is known in Ireland as *Cogadh an Dá Rí*, or
the War of the Two Kings.

Also known as the Williamite War in Ireland, it was
sparked off when the Stuart monarch James II, under threat
from powerful factions who feared a return to the
dominance of Roman Catholicism under his rule, fled into
French exile.

The Protestant William of Orange and his wife Mary
were invited to take up the thrones of Scotland, Ireland and
England – but James had significant Catholic support in
Ireland.

His supporters were known as Jacobites, and Rooneys
were among their ranks.

Ireland became the battleground for an ultimately
abortive attempt to restore James to his throne, and after
much slaughter on both sides the Jacobites were forced to
surrender in September of 1691.

A peace treaty known as the Treaty of Limerick
followed, under which those willing to swear an oath of
loyalty to William were allowed to remain in their native
land.

Those reluctant to do so, including many Rooneys,
chose foreign exile – their ancient homelands lost to them
forever.

Chapter four:

On the world stage

**Bearers of the Rooney name have excelled in a colourful
variety of pursuits, and no less so than in the highly
competitive world of sport.**

One of the most gifted footballers of his generation,
Wayne Rooney is the English striker who was born in 1985
in the Croxteth district of Liverpool.

He grew up supporting his local club Everton, and it was
to this club that he signed on schoolboy terms at the age of
only ten.

He scored a match-winning goal for Everton against
the then reigning league champions Arsenal when he was
only five days short of his 17th birthday, making him then
the youngest goal scorer in English Premier League
history.

Named BBC Sports' 2002-2003 Young Personality of
the Year, he signed from Everton to Manchester United in
August of 2004 in a £31m deal.

This, at the time, was the most expensive transfer for a
teenage player, because he was only a few weeks from his
19th birthday.

Still playing for Manchester United at the time of
writing, he has also been a member of the England national
team since 2003.

Also in European football, **Adam Rooney** is the Irish striker who was born in 1988 in Dublin. At the time of writing he plays for Scottish Premier League Club Inverness Caledonian Thistle, having signed from Stoke City.

His older brother, **Mark Rooney,** is also a talented footballer, playing at the time of writing in the Football League of Ireland with Shelbourne.

In the swimming pool, **Giann Rooney** is the Australian swimmer who was born in 1982 in Brisbane.

Competing for her nation at the 1998 Commonwealth Games, she won a gold medal in the 100-metres backstroke and was also part of the gold-winning team in the 4x100-metres medley relay event.

She was also part of the Australian team that won a gold medal in the women's 4x100-metres medley relay at the 2004 Olympics in Athens.

In baseball, **John Rooney** is the American sports pundit born in 1954 in Richmond, Missouri, who is a popular radio broadcaster for the St. Louis Cardinals.

He worked previous to this as a sportscaster for CBS Radio.

On the athletics track, **Martin Rooney** is the English sprinter who was born in 1987 in Thornton Heath, London, and who began running for the Croydon Harriers.

Winner of the bronze medal in the 400-metres event at the 2006 World Junior Championships, he won gold in the 2005 European Juniors relay event.

In volleyball, **Sean Rooney**, born in 1982 in Wheaton, Illinois, is the American indoor volleyball player who plays as an outside hitter for the U.S. National Team and who was a member of the team that took gold in the 2008 Olympics in Beijing.

In the rough and tumble that is the game of rugby, **Jamie Rooney** is the English rugby union stand-off, scrum-half and England international who was born in 1980 in Featherstone, Yorkshire.

In American football, **Art Rooney** was the founding owner of the famed Pittsburgh Steelers franchise in the National Football League. Born in 1901 in Pittsburgh, the son of Irish immigrant parents from Newry, Co. Down, it was in 1933 that he used $2,500 he had won on horse racing to pay the required National Football League franchise fee for a club based in his home city.

He named the club the Pirates, renamed as the Pittsburgh Steelers in 1942.

Rooney, who died in 1988, was the father of **Dan Rooney**, the present owner and chairman of the Pittsburgh Steelers.

Born in the city in 1932, he is responsible for what is known as Rooney's Law – a requirement for National Football League teams with coaching and general manager vacancies to interview at least one candidate from a minority background.

Proud of his Irish roots, he is also the founder of the

Rooney Prize for Irish Literature, awarded annually to published Irish writers aged under 40.

Previous recipients of the award include Desmond Hogan, Kate Cruise O'Brien and, in 2008, Leontia Flynn for her collection of poems *Drives*.

Also in the creative world of the written and spoken word, **Andy Rooney** is the veteran American radio and television writer who was born in 1919 in Albany, New York.

His career began in journalism when, drafted into the U.S. Army during the Second World War, be became a correspondent for the forces' newspaper *Stars and Stripes*.

In February of 1943 he was one of six journalists who flew with the U.S Eighth Air Force on its first bombing raid over Germany, while he was also one of the first American journalists to visit and report on the horrors of the newly liberated Nazi concentration camps.

His war experiences form the basis of his memoir *My War*.

He joined CBS Radio as a writer in 1949,while his first television 'essay' was written in 1964.

His weekly *A Few Minutes with Andy Rooney* has formed an integral part of the CBS television news programme *60 Minutes* since 1978, while he also has a syndicated news column that appears in many newspapers across the United States.

The recipient of no less than three Emmy awards for his television essays, he is also the recipient of a Lifetime Achievement Emmy.

His books and collections of essays include the 1991 *Sincerely, Andy Rooney*, the 2002 *Common Nonsense*, the 2003 *Years of Minutes* and, from 2006, *Out of My Mind*.

Born in Dublin in 1840, **Teresa J. Rooney** was the Irish writer who died in 1911 and whose works include the 1880 The *Last Monarch of Tara* and the 1909 *The Strike*, while **Philip Rooney** was the noted novelist and scriptwriter whose novels include the 1946 *Captain Boycott* and the 1949 *The Quest for Matt Talbot*.

Born in Sligo in 1907, he died in 1966.

Bearers of the Rooney name have also been, and continue to be, prominent in the political arena.

Born in 1950, **Terence Rooney** is the British Labour MP for Bradford North and who, at the time of writing, is the only member of The Church of Jesus Christ of Latter-day Saints – better known as the Mormons – to sit in the House of Commons.

In the United States, **John J. Rooney** was the Democrat politician born in 1903 who served as assistant district attorney in Brooklyn, New York, from 1940 to 1944 – the year in which he was elected to the U.S. Congress.

He died in 1975.

In the sphere of social activism, **J. Patrick Rooney**, born in 1928 and who died in 2008, was the founder and chairman of America's Fairness Foundation, an organisation dedicated to helping low income families with health care and education.

In the world of contemporary music, **Rooney** is the five-piece rock band from Los Angeles named after the school principal character Ed Rooney in the film *Ferris Bueller's Day Off*.

First formed in 1999, their albums include the 2003 *Rooney* and the 2007 *Calling the World*.

One of the most famous bearers of the Rooney name is someone who was actually born Joseph Yule Jr.

This is the veteran American actor and entertainer better known by his stage name of **Mickey Rooney**.

Born in 1920 in Brooklyn, New York his father was Joseph Yule, an immigrant from Scotland, while his mother Nellie hailed from Kansas City.

His parents were vaudeville artists and the young Joseph Yule, later to achieve fame as Mickey Rooney, made his first stage appearance with them at the age of only 15 months in a specially tailored tuxedo.

His first film role came at the age of five in the *Mickey McGuire* series of short films, while from 1937 to 1946 he starred in the *Andy Hardy* series of films.

During a break in the filming of the series in 1932, his mother decided to capitalise on her son's popularity by taking him on a ten-week vaudeville tour of America, billed as 'Mickey McGuire'.

But the film studio threatened a lawsuit, claiming it held copyright on the name.

The matter of young Joe Yule's stage name was finally resolved when he opted for Mickey Rooney – in preference to his mother's suggestion, in view of his comedy antics, of Mickey Looney.

His first major film role was opposite Judy Garland in the 1937 *Thoroughbreds Don't Cry*, while he performed to critical dramatic acclaim in the 1938 *Boy's Town*, opposite Spencer Tracy.

Both Rooney and Garland, meanwhile, became a successful song and dance team, most notably in the 1939 Oscar-nominated *Babes in Arms*. The recipient of an Oscar Juvenile Award in 1938, he was also awarded an Honorary Oscar in 1983 for his lifetime achievement.

Described by the late British actor Laurence Olivier as 'the single best film actor America had ever produced', among his many other films are the 1961 *Breakfast at Tiffany's*, the 2006 *Night at the Museum* and the 2008 *Driving Me Crazy*.

Married eight times, including to the actress Ava Gardner from 1942 to 1943, Rooney has been married since 1978 to Jan Chamberlin – with whom he tours in the live stage production *Let's Put on a Show!*

In 2007, the irrepressible actor made his British pantomime debut when he played Baron Hardup in *Cinderella* at the Sunderland Empire Theatre.

At the time of writing he holds the Guinness Book of Records' accolade as the actor with the longest career on both stage and screen.

Even the animal world has produced a famous bearer of the Rooney name – in the four-legged form of the champion American thoroughbred racehorse **Princess Rooney**.

Born in 1980 and beginning her spectacular three-year racing career at the age of two, she won practically all of her races, including the Kentucky Oaks.

Princess Rooney died in comfortable retirement in 2008, seventeen years after being inducted into the United States' National Museum of Racing and Hall of Fame.

Key dates in Ireland's history from the first settlers to the formation of the Irish Republic:

circa 7000 B.C.	Arrival and settlement of Stone Age people.
circa 3000 B.C.	Arrival of settlers of New Stone Age period.
circa 600 B.C.	First arrival of the Celts.
200 A.D.	Establishment of Hill of Tara, Co. Meath, as seat of the High Kings.
circa 432 A.D.	Christian mission of St. Patrick.
800-920 A.D.	Invasion and subsequent settlement of Vikings.
1002 A.D.	Brian Boru recognised as High King.
1014	Brian Boru killed at battle of Clontarf.
1169-1170	Cambro-Norman invasion of the island.
1171	Henry II claims Ireland for the English Crown.
1366	Statutes of Kilkenny ban marriage between native Irish and English.
1529-1536	England's Henry VIII embarks on religious Reformation.
1536	Earl of Kildare rebels against the Crown.
1541	Henry VIII declared King of Ireland.
1558	Accession to English throne of Elizabeth I.
1565	Battle of Affane.
1569-1573	First Desmond Rebellion.
1579-1583	Second Desmond Rebellion.
1594-1603	Nine Years War.
1606	Plantation' of Scottish and English settlers.
1607	Flight of the Earls.
1632-1636	Annals of the Four Masters compiled.
1641	Rebellion over policy of plantation and other grievances.
1649	Beginning of Cromwellian conquest.
1688	Flight into exile in France of Catholic Stuart monarch James II as Protestant Prince William of Orange invited to take throne of England along with his wife, Mary.
1689	William and Mary enthroned as joint monarchs; siege of Derry.
1690	Jacobite forces of James defeated by William at battle of the Boyne (July) and Dublin taken.

1691	Athlone taken by William; Jacobite defeats follow at Aughrim, Galway, and Limerick; conflict ends with Treaty of Limerick (October) and Irish officers allowed to leave for France.
1695	Penal laws introduced to restrict rights of Catholics; banishment of Catholic clergy.
1704	Laws introduced constricting rights of Catholics in landholding and public office.
1728	Franchise removed from Catholics.
1791	Foundation of United Irishmen republican movement.
1796	French invasion force lands in Bantry Bay.
1798	Defeat of Rising in Wexford and death of United Irishmen leaders Wolfe Tone and Lord Edward Fitzgerald.
1800	Act of Union between England and Ireland.
1803	Dublin Rising under Robert Emmet.
1829	Catholics allowed to sit in Parliament.
1845-1849	The Great Hunger: thousands starve to death as potato crop fails and thousands more emigrate.
1856	Phoenix Society founded.
1858	Irish Republican Brotherhood established.
1873	Foundation of Home Rule League.
1893	Foundation of Gaelic League.
1904	Foundation of Irish Reform Association.
1913	Dublin strikes and lockout.
1916	Easter Rising in Dublin and proclamation of an Irish Republic.
1917	Irish Parliament formed after Sinn Fein election victory.
1919-1921	War between Irish Republican Army and British Army.
1922	Irish Free State founded, while six northern counties remain part of United Kingdom as Northern Ireland, or Ulster; civil war up until 1923 between rival republican groups.
1949	Foundation of Irish Republic after all remaining constitutional links with Britain are severed.